SILKY THEFTS

SILKY THEFTS

MICHAEL JENNINGS

For Dr. Petters —
A book of bones
Michael J
1/2008

ORCHISES

WASHINGTON

2007

Library of Congress Cataloging in Publication Data

Jennings, Michael, 1948-
  Silky thefts / Michael Jennings.
    p. cm.
  ISBN-13: 978-1-932535-12-9 (alk. paper)
    I. Title

PS3560.E525S55 2007
811'.54—dc22

2006049358

ACKNOWLEDGEMENTS

Special thanks to the *Vanderbilt Review* for publishing "Heat" and to Pine Press for publishing the chapbook *A Dance of Stone* that contained the same poem. Thanks also to *Comstock Review* for publishing "Remains" and to Pine Press for publishing the chapbook *Ghost Moon* that also included this poem.

I would like to acknowledge Rome Arts Center for their second place award to "Old Mountains" in the 2001 Milton Dorfman Poetry Prize contest. In 2003, both "Old Mountains" and "Remains" were translated into Lithuanian by Sonata Paliulyte and appeared in *Literatura ir means,* a cultural weekly published in Vilnius.

A final note of thanks to Daniel Hoffman for valuable advice and encouragement and to my wife Suzanne Shane for her tireless support and critical insight.

Orchises Press
P. O. Box 20602
Alexandria, Virginia, 22320-1602

G6E4C2A

for

Suzanne

and

Shane

CONTENTS

UR OF THE CHALDEES, 1958

They are like aliens on the moon, the Americans—
bermuda shorts and cameras, pudgy, pale,
a little queasy from the train ride.
Dust from the storm in the night
has permeated everything they own
down to the skin.
They are not quite certain why they came,
and wear the baffled, blinking looks of baby birds.

The hole in the ground is the biggest I've ever seen,
with "evidence of the flood"—a four-foot wide ribbon
of sand half way up the sides of an otherwise brown pit
strewn with broken bits of pottery. Local kids, urchins,
scamper down the steep, thin path at break-neck speed
for *rials* and *dinars*. They seem to have sprung up here
without benefit of parents or care. Across
the millennia, I feel the closeness of children
and the terrible price of money.

After a long climb, I am first to reach the summit
of the ziggurat
and so enter the dusky sky of Abraham.
I am 10. My heart is a drum.
I stand at the top of the god-forsaken world.

HEAT

Day without plot. Fixtured and fissured. Fractured beyond measure.

I have known heat to stretch horizon to horizon
Like bright steel—a metal or mica or star-scattered heaven
Foundering the mind. Thick-tongued and wordless. White sand
On black brain. Blood rivered in suet. A pocket
Picked empty as wind.
                                        Nothing moves in such heat,
Not lizard or scorpion, sandfly or shadow. Tree
Becomes rock, becomes gray husk, becomes
Ruinous. Squalor of sand. Numbness of sun.
                                                        To squat there,
The stones of your absence in your hands,
Is to squat in the center of silence forever.
It is to hold the sun like water in the crumbling of your hands.

It is to hold the bright day. Sun. Sand. A dun-colored dog

Disappearing into a distance of sun and sand—
Humped, slavering. The steady
Rise and fall of the four flickering paws
Too maniacally silent and concentrated for even
The loose gesture of wind to intrude on.
                              Or the dream of the day,
A child's sorrowing and dreaming—aftermath
Of that too much excitement. Four boys with baseball bats
Who had braved what they knew of the horrors
Of the desert, a compound of mad dogs
And oil drums,
              barbed wire and heat,
A dun-colored dog disappearing into desert like a dead wind.

It hangs like a daydream of fish in the sun's eye. Fish flying

Like birds above the thunder of dynamite, burble of river,
Then falling to flotsam. Fish by the armload,
Blind, dazed, flaccid as faith. A stench
Ripping open the whole length of the gullet of sky
And left for foxes and flies.
                            A day I walked in sun
Unstable as the dynamite I carried in a brown paper sack
Like an indigestible lunch.
                            And threw. And walked. And threw.
And watched the shards of hillside rise
Like torn brains to hang in the hair of scrub-trees
While the lizard sang silent in the sun—the blood-
Throated lizard, bloated and bragging in the swaggering sun.

Or the daydream of glass. White light. Bone light. The sailing of glass—

Shards of pottery heaped in domes
Where ziggurats grew round in wind
And the tombs of kings
Stunk with centuries of fox.
                              The sun was a blind mad eye
Carved on an obsidian stairway to heaven
Where the fallen bulls of stone
Offered their great backs to me to ride
And dust filled the air like glass.
                              Mother's eyes were black fires
As she hurled ashtrays and plates, bowls and crystal
At walls and mirrors. Her voice
Was glass breaking. Her breath was ether.
                              The stench of fox,
Like the burning of flesh, stayed in my nostrils for days.

A dream before I knew you, met you. Though I knew of your absence.

I knew of Lydia Cathcart who spread her great thighs
On the Riding Club couch or across
The great outcropped boulders of the desert
For grooms and stablehands.
                              I knew of her husband's
Straw-colored pomaded hair and creased
High-fashion trousers,
                              and how her eyes bugged out a little
And spittle formed at the edges of her mouth.
                                             Akbar,
Who would die in the advanced stages of syphilis,
Served our drinks and food, laughed
Like a girl, and kissed me when he could.
I knew of your absence. And I dreamed of Lydia Cathcart.

And of women on horseback—long shadows in the deep hills.

And one who rode a stallion like a black wind
That even I could not ride,
                         her hair a raven black.
And then the horse who fell and bled for me,
A deep pocket of blood forming between his forelegs
Like a breast—
                 a black horse with a girl's mane
And a king's name.
                     And then the dream of women
Ridden by men or boys
In the twilit paddock, moving
Down the long hill in the long heat, arm
In arm, indifferent to all but the long loneliness
Of the first stars rising,
                     the glittering of raw, fierce weapons.

And the desert rises then in the twilight. It lifts

Its burnt body out of itself. The scabs of its flesh
Soften. It sings in its silence like an old woman
And becomes young again.

                                            Her sands glitter in moonlight.
Her ridges rise like deep rivers entering the sea of stars.
Her foxes find new stealth,

                         their fur bristles.
Snakes slither from dark dens with eyes like stars
And tongues like the singing of stars.

                                    This is the clarity
Of fire.

              This is the clarity of the long bones of the hills
Rubbing together like the thighs of the long women
Buried among them.

                        This is death.
This is the white-hot crotch of death, blue as a diamond.

And Gafoor smokes his hookah with yellow eyes. Rocks

And claps his thighs. Dreams himself. Stinks of horse,
Stinks of women, stinks of the sun and the sun's lies,
The long ride.
                    And the round stones of the moonlight
Are the hunched backs of the night's feeders
Who rise and walk—
                    Or the arched bellies of the night's
Eaten. Who do not get up. Who turn on themselves
Like sculpture. Blue stones.
                    And the tarantula
Rising like smoke
                    sings to his green-eyed mate
Under the arched light of her dark sting,
And dances there in the round light.
                    Long night.
The yellow-eyed. Soft-thighed. Torn and turning.

And then shard-light in the broken east and the stones' cry—

The huddled bones,
Carcass and carcass. Confession of sand,
Celebration of wind.

               And bright blood blooms in the desert
As the blind white fish
Flounder from withered pond
To withered pond
Where once the river flowed hard
In the moonlight.

         Achilles died
That Odysseus might live—the heartless heart
Succumbing to the body's stealth,

                 the moon-fired fox,
Skulking and singing, meeting the dawn's dead eye.

O daughter of days. Mother of nights. If I have sought women

As the sun
Seeks water,

        eye
In eye,

     tear

        and muscle,

                forgive me the long chains'
Shackle and shackle. Forgive me the great bull-bones
Of the world in the sun,

                and hold me now in the implacable
Pallor of your gaze, this improbable poise
Of full moon at dawn's edge—

               Bone-song,

                     wind-haunt,

Voice of the fathers
And the father of voice—

           Bring back
The great wind,

       sing me the singing,

              the great song—

O blood of the mothers who labored long!

OLD MOUNTAINS

There were mountains in the old place,
the place of old bones, and the mountains
were like bones, only browner, sandstone,
though sometimes bleached pale as bones.
And dark goats moved among them,
and the people who grew out of them
were like goats, small and dark
and quick when the sun was not pure
poison, moving about their business
which was not our business, theirs
being soil, which there wasn't much of,
ours being oil, which came out of the ground
by the ton and snaked through the hills
and desert in pipelines inevitable
as the azure, steel sky itself. Perhaps
they were not real mountains so much
as up-thrust foothills, craggy plateau
a man or goat could climb in a day,
stand at the top of, and feel Moses
come down from.
                    They were holy mountains,
and under the holy mountains was oil
that sometimes still made bushes burn
or the Red Sea part for the islands
of deep-bellied freighters, pregnant
with crude.

And if they were not mountains,
they were at least the high steppes
of the horsemen, grown ghostly with time,
and my sleeper's body slept among them,
and my dreamer's body, which was only smoke
from village chimneys in winter, or the black
eyes of the skulls of their huts in summer,
saw the quick shimmering emerald of the fields
and crevices in spring, the flash of the bright-dressed
girls of the waterhole, their ankle bracelets
saucy as the glitter of crime in Salome's eyes,
and the black eyes under the black wind
of the black *chadora*
billowing around the husks of crones.
They were the sacred mountains camped
at our outskirts, while our fathers
mined oil from beneath them and hardly
saw them.
                    But their graves sang to us
in the evenings, and the thin smoke
of their cook-fires rose like ghosts,
and they lay down with us in our dreams
like beasts, breathing and patient.
                                        "Ours,"
we thought, as the Persian blue sky
swaddled their shoulders, as the black
night sky lay down on their backs

with its pinprick stars. They rose
like continents in the black sea
of nightfall, then rose again like the skulls
of sacrificial beasts in the dawn. And perhaps
our white mothers heard them and started
drinking harder, savaging the servants,
quarreling with our sad-sack fathers.
Distracted in the midnight, they paced cold tiles,
their bare feet lisping the hours—
ethereal, haughty, silken whisperings.
And the mountains were theirs, too,
and the dirty hands of the servants
who needed such scolding. Some absence
lurked in their eyes like the shadows
of mountains, among the coffee klatches
and beer-swilling mornings.

But we
were the children of the mountains,
and they entered us as easily as sky,
as easily as night, and what they showed us
was fire and shadow, dancers under the worn moon.
And we saw how time moved in ripples toward the horizon,
shuddering under the noonday sun. They moved
in us like the spirits of Alexander or Herod,
Nebuchadnezzar, Ashurbanipal, Xerxes
or Ataxerxes—slow fires
in the waking midnight.

And our incongruous
fathers waited at the bus stop—white,
short-sleeved shirts, clip-on ties
and crew cuts. They talked of Oklahoma
or L.A., Atlantic City or Baton Rouge,
but never of the bleached mountains
on the hem of whose skirts they stood
dazed in the morning light. Their gaze
was too calculated, the sheaves of paper
in their briefcases too diagrammatic
and impersonal. Children of the Depression,
their souls had suffered foreclosure.
They had bankers' eyes.

                    They are mostly
dead now, copies of *Forbes Magazine*
strewn on the night table. And we
who were children of the mountains
search nightly on the News for glimpses
of the pale, pitiless sleepers—there
behind the reporter with blank banker's eyes,
beyond the rolling dust of tanks, bomb blasts
and squalor, the rubble of apocalypse.
We have joined the absent ones.
Nothing there now remembers us but the mountains
etched behind our eyelids.

ALEX

(1929-2001)

1.

No act of will or Psychic Hotline cant
can raise you from the "utility urn"
I bought you in from Jern's Crematorium
last week. You're done, Mom, and you shan't
correct my English, nor nothing rail nor rant
against forever more. No high-dudgeon
antics can stir the pot. Not even Nieman
Marcus on credit card can make you less than spent.
Farewell to the 12 Minton place settings
you never used, and to the Stickley bed
big as a Roman bath—to the nightshade
and St. John's Wort, masseuse, bed-wettings,
panic calls, blindness—all that pricey dread—
and those who promised love that never came.

2.

You were of course the damaged princess, downed
at seven by the osteomyelitis
in your forehead—surgery, leeches,
one eyelid frozen, headaches that would pound
and pound until you saw yourself as drowned
and then redeemed in your own helplessness.
Great doctors mumbled over you like priests
until the divorce lawyers came and found
your miscarrying mother drug addicted,
your rich daddy a secret queer and crazy.
The baffled judge at last left you to choose.
You were just 10. Your breathing grew constricted
and the courtroom walls leaned in. You told me
how the strange tears splashed on your new red shoes.

3.

And so you chose the mother you would hate
by 17, who stole your friends and lied
and put on airs, while the new poverty tied
you to yourself like a bad smell. Late
to work one morning in the Gulf Coast heat
after a six mile walk, you were mortified
to find deodorant on your desk, tied
up with a little ribbon of pure hate.
That was the day, perhaps, you swore off sweat.
Powdered, perfumed, your beauty cool as ice,
you wore a long red coat, stiletto heels.
When, like soft wind, you tucked me in at night
and whisked away into a world of eyes
and mouths and random men, I felt your steel.

4.

I hear your sniff of violated privacy
as my man's hands riffle the soft innards
of your long bureaus—folded, layered,
immaculate, lush femininity,
but not quite lacy—wombs of secrecy
that hold old letters in frayed ribbons, half-heard
snatches of conversation like the words
of little girls whose coy hypocrisy
you loathed. Was it your father's shortness made
you crave tall men, with timber in their voices,
who glowered down at me like men on stilts.
Was it just irony the man you married
stood only five foot six and favored boys.
Still I hear the venom of your hissing silks.

5.

"Jarvis, Elizabeth Alice," your great
grandmother, slips from a bottom drawer,
faded but lovely as a long-pressed flower,
at perhaps 17. I contemplate
her unstrung collar. She was maybe late
to come in for the photo session hour,
her hair windblown, a breathless now or
never slight parting of the lips. Her fate
was to become an itinerant schoolmarm,
revered for high intelligence and wit,
who married a young minister and raised
three daughters of a certain bearing, charm,
humor and piety. What doesn't quite fit
the story, though, are her eyes—wild, slightly crazed.

6.

What tamed that wild gaze that did not tame yours—
the cold Michigan farm? — anxieties
by candlelight?—the sleepless ministries
to endless household needs? From bottom drawers
they all come tumbling out, the ancestor
church ladies. Your grandmother's diaries,
chock full of weather's cheery godliness,
tell nothing of herself, only her prayers
to better serve. They warmed the glittering ice
of those heartbreaking farms that made you cringe,
if family jottings be believed. White-haired,
bleak-boned daughters of the mad-eyed Alice,
they show up faded at the faded edges
of family picnics—wistful, shyly proud.

7.

Your existential loathing of the family
tree came early. One minister seduced
proved quite enough. Even old "Elder" Brewster
of the Mayflower hung there in the leafy
branches your mother grew like Blake's Poison Tree.
Its roots were Charlemagne and Robert Bruce,
the Black Douglas and John of Gaunt. No half-truth
was squandered in her quest for ancestry
of might and merit. You were the poor daughter
who'd never measure up to that high-flown bunk
and didn't try. You sang your own mantra.
You were no Mary Ann, let alone "Junior."
You were no pious chip off the old stump.
You changed your name to Alexandra.

8.

Not the carpool mother who sang I Like
Ike songs. Not the girl damaged by her father
who could not say no but not quite yes either.
Not she who made little me one May night
with a blond Mick prize-fighter without quite
conceiving what went on in the weeds there.
Not the petulant, angry daughter,
or even the bad mother or bad wife.
You wanted to exist uncategorically.
You wanted to be an original
created in the diamond moment. Not
for you the pain of being only
one woman. You desired to be impossible,
and stirred and stirred and stirred and stirred the pot.

9.

You loathed your mother's wheeler-dealer lies.
She worried you could *be* but could not do—
and always two stories of what was true—
yours and hers, hers and yours in perfect symmetry—
her outward quest, your inward journey,
clashing like cymbals. Both your winds could woo
me. I just saw varying shades of blue—
you darker and she lighter, but the same sea.
You both loved words, and words kept you apart.
In the same room, I'd feel your grinding wills
like creaking oarlocks, both a little crazy
and both killed off by the same bad heart.
You read Proust. She read me Wordsworth's "Daffodils."
In different climes, you each got called "a lady."

10.

You toyed with me with threats of suicide

that year I turned 11. Even then

I thought you were just putting me on

at least half the time. But of course I cried

and rubbed your back, and in my own way tried

to wrestle down your darkest demons

as if you were my double. And just once

I feared you'd kill me in my sleep—some tired

hotel in Switzerland as I recall.

We'd fought. You had been drinking pretty hard.

But I remember mostly how the lake

was blue as lapis and we were immortal.

The incident left us drifting apart.

We just let it alone for beauty's sake.

11.

All family wars play out best with three.
"What can we do with Alex, what's anyone
to do with Alex," Grandmother would intone
when I was fourteen and thought life easy.
We'd settle in for a long night's breezy
confession of your sins. Crazy as a loon
sometimes, she had the storyteller's one
virtue—to forge some actuality
just as she forged diplomas that got her work.
You were the poor poet of introverted
glances, who saw not things but in their ideas
that fluttered mothily toward the Absurd.
For you communion lurked behind the words.
After dissecting you, we'd have our *brioche.*

12.

You showed no great interest in your grandson
and hated any grandmotherly role.
The very appellation seemed to appall
you, as if threatening your sense of fashion
and proper distance. No cuddly fat munchkin
hugger you. It was all about control
and self-possession and your ghastly will.
The touch you craved was near another ocean
under the calm fingers of your masseuse.
What you could buy you could put trust in—
even to that huge, sombre library
whose books you never bothered to peruse.
You were just out there like the last Victorian
dying amidst some phantom tea party.

13.

With enough money nothing need be real.
You blew through seven hundred thousand,
a grand a month for your group psychic plan
alone. The rest, just baubles of the *haute* genteel—
Cartier clocks, drawers full of identical
designer suits in three sizes, not one
worn—scarves and sweaters numberless as sand,
and so on. Mostly it was pretty dismal
being you those last years, ordering things
through UPS to have a moment's friend
when packages arrived. Your eyes were failing
and liver functions—clear rememberings
of things that had not ever happened.
The sirens in your blood-starved head were wailing.

14.

When it was clear the money had run out,
quite willessly you fell upon your sword,
refusing Laesix that your doctor ordered
and losing him for that. For one coquette
moment you tried to call a quick about
face, change your mind. Nurses were guarded—
it was too late now for that. You looked bored
and drifted back to sleep. And that was that.
Your new-friend cosmetician held your hand.
Another startled as she entered your room
and one bright blue eye held her in its death-chill.
There was no code blue or shenanigans.
You'd become bride to yet another groom.
The angry child kicking in your head lay still.

15.

Your portraits we brought home filled several boxes—
from Shirley Temple days to the young Hepburn,
your slightly cocked head and cocked eyebrow turn
the gaze inward, despite the outward glances
at the demanding camera. Long eyelashes
veil the quick bright eye. Something flickers and burns
and smolders out. A certain porcelain
veneer distracts us from your beauty's darkness.
What you held dearest was your inner kingdom.
In most all of the portraits, that shows up.
None of them hold the look I cherish—
that devil-may-care, slightly-over-the-top,
what-the-hell grin. That wink. It all said come
dance, little broody boy, it's all there is.

REMAINS

My son guides me up the long hill
squelching in run-off, along trails
narrow as goat paths through the trees
to show me the strewn bones of a deer
nested in her shed shreds of fur,
almost golden, where some wood spirit
laid her to rest, and the coyotes
and crows stripped her, leaving only
a hoof and furred knuckle intact
among a clutter of collapsed ribs.
He shows me the clean white vertebrae,
the pelvis with its odd eye hole,
the knee still attached with some last rope
of sinew.
              This is his find, stumbled on
as he tried his new spring legs in a downhill,
helter-skelter run, and stopped, and stared,
and in his eleven year old mind knew
that this was the stuff of running
undone, something the receding snow
left for him personally, a sign
of winter's weight.
                        We eye it together.
We go down on our knees to gather pieces
of the witchcraft mystery. The grey trees

around us are also bones that click
and chatter in the wet wind
of almost spring. The brown limpid eyes
are gone. The crumbling gnarl
of spine, once nerved and tremulous,
is now only a train wreck the grass
will hide in a month's time. We feel
the doorway of earth opening.
We feel the thinness of our skins
and the prickling of short hairs rising.
We know what's at the bottom of things,
how soon the mayflies will be dancing
their measured reels of the evening.

INVOCATIONS

My steps slower than I would have imagined
even in summer

who once could not help but run
Crimes I've done myself I would not undo

Cicadas in a tree singing
the dappled "out there"

the shrill of birdsong

*   *   *   *

Sands of the desert and sun warm me
and I forgive my pederast father
and remember his shy laugh

Spawn of East Texas swamps snakes on the brain
Stink of rot and piney woods loneliness
Bible-belt mom dowsed in lavender

I had an engineer's hat like my grandfather's
high in the sun-flared locomotive squinting into the light

the two of us until the whistle blew
and he was a crouched old man on a hospital inner tube

My father's bones shattered like glass and he died
worse than a dog so I forgave him

remembering his shy laugh glints of gold
in his long old teeth

Two funny stories maybe three and no one knew him
His skull in death an old Ojibwa's
*   *   *   *

At night the familiar hocus pocus of moon and mind
You soft in shadow that other
I know myself by

Come Light warm me
Sit on my grandmother's shoulder
who reads me through measles and chickenpox
bringing the world and New Orleans
in two blue suitcases

Light on the banana tree tallest of grasses
Light in her hazel eyes
*   *   *   *

Salt sand of the desert the long unfolding white of it
Out there I stole my bride from the land of the untouchables
Spirit me away dawn of the cockcrow
Light of my wavering window
*   *   *   *

My one great photograph you naked on a chaise lounge
eight months pregnant sleeping in the sun
light circling your circles
and one long draped arm

Light of the moment and always
*   *   *   *

Our son came out a greased chicken when he was born
and shone in the light of all subsequent Christmases

He seemed too small to take home
I had to learn to hold his head up

Your breasts engorged made you the gaudy
fertility goddess carved on a wooden salad spoon
I remembered from childhood

I gave him his first bath
Danced him heart to heart
Happy on the high hill of our summer
*   *   *   *

And happily I am already dead in a book somewhere
but in the dark closed pages or the light of a window
I don't know

To think I was ever a blank page
a tabula rasa a salt flat
a star

Hold the light at the window I am coming
though my knees ache

*   *   *   *

I have always enjoyed near the Equator
how sun maps a face
though I live in the snow

I was young in the sun of tennis courts
Pure form and goat mind
fencing the air

before the flat-light green-haze of hospitals
moonmen in surgeries
Mother a mirage in the midnight
arriving from Rome

Stars of Paris outside my window
the girl I held in the dark for 13 years
against my loneliness
swims in the sun of the Pacific now
or is dead

*   *   *   *

I made love on a red cliff over the Mediterranean
at midnight in the cove of Los Pinos
to a woman from another language
beautiful as a mermaid
and hairy as a 23 year old
I was young dumb in a hurry

No star touched my soul

*   *   *   *

When I think of light I think of salt flats or snow
though its jewels in the leaves are delectable
and fire your black hair

All these summers I've watched you garden our gold hill
Your hillocks not bad Old Woman
raised like prayer

Names of flowers elude me unless I look them up
Is it the desert in me or a dark mind
that cannot name these belles of light

My first garden was elephant ears and banana trees
and blunt-nosed tortoises I kissed on their blunt noses
mossy bricks of the patio
a slight breeze I still recall
on my heat-rashed two-year-old naked buttocks

At three and a ward of the Church
I wanted to bathe with the Deacon's
13 year old daughter Mary Katherine
because I liked her pubic hair
how it swirled in the warm water

One or two baths and everyone thought better of it
From then on it was Morgan or Hank

And still my life seems strange
I think my lake the Danube sometimes
or remember the pale lime-thick turquoise of the Karoon River
an eel under my left foot
in a shock of wonder

Salt flats and snow and the gardens between
*   *   *   *

Wherever it was light wanted to go
I said Yo Dis here is America
Let's do-si-do
Dat old Walt Whitman he big he kind
but boring

Which tribe am I
The twang the drawl the Yankee clipper
Which thrum of weathers
Which codes and netherworlds
Which beestings on the tongue

Or is the eye my alibi
and crude syntax
*   *   *   *

The eye that travels
sees still waves from airplanes

thunderless beaches

In the border towns
of the dead and nearly dead
comes dawn's bleak windows

The casualties were
entirely justified
say the generals

And all that flat line clarity is light

But what of the gutturals of evening
the festooned flesh and ornamental slang
the topsy-turvy muscles of a million mutabilities
carnal carnivals and carnivores
boardwalk bazaar bodega
heartstrings of the tongue's thrumming

when light of the blood is a kind of light
   *   *   *   *

I drummed through the booze jungles of Bangkok
at age 15 door to door whore to whore
till one just 17 took me home to meet the folks
and wash me in the kitchen sink
It was intimate chilling a grim mirror
and in the sickly light of the bare bulb
she was truly beautiful

How much of her may have wished to dance
on my grave I don't know

*   *   *   *

Angels and vaginas the angels are
vaginas says my sculptor friend in his studio
when I find his new seraphim
stock and static

Stepping back I see it
Yes
if thighs had wings surely we could fly

From a dark declivity a few curlings
broadening into fern fronds
and baroque arabesques
a vertical mouth for a trunk
and the tree of life is any man's wife

*   *   *   *

And then there were the horses of the sun
ablaze over the clattering rooftops of the world
or at least Khuzistan with its rock hills
and smugglers' trails
A heartbeat between the knees
A breathing like the very wind
Flying the flags of themselves in their girlish manes
the foolishness of all our fathers in their wild eyes

In a monoprint I bought from a friend

three horses graze in a pasture

that might be cloud

the passionless horses of dream or a far field

closer to me now than the horses of wind and fire

muscle and bone

though I miss their salt scent

the rivers of sweat mapping the veins of their necks

Or maybe my friend's print is a dream of horses

dreaming their pastures dreaming their clouds

dreaming the artist dreaming of horses

whose absence is light

around the dark remembered bodies

*   *   *   *

When my horse the fastest in all Khuzistan died

I was away at college and knew in an instant

my childhood had ended

I tried writing a poem

but couldn't get the braille of his skin

under my fingers onto the page

He'd lent me the great thunder of his body

and I had lain on his flanks in his stall while he slept

We loved each other with humor like brothers

On the day of our triumph he had blown by

Star of Persia to win by 20 lengths

He nickered and snorted when he heard my footsteps

and when I did not come for months he died

His life blessed mine as only animals can bless
Sometimes our betrayals are mindless as wind
and a man moves emptier than the child that had been

*   *   *   *

Moon of my mind with your long black hair
Come nearer sit opposite
Let me paint you the girl in the rattan chair
one full breast exposed
one knee drawn up that hides the other
A portrait in shadow but the light of the room

Or now the wise handsome woman Penelope old
whom Odysseus fears taking his eyes off
in his fog of years
The firm cool cheek and coolish eyes
and fires that flicker at night
along her spine

Flesh is not sexy to an old man's eye
until defied by gravity the slightly
slipped buttocks that affirms some pride
the waist loosening its stays
that still has grace
the back that arches that's known some ache
Of course it helps he knew the girl
entwined back in that Ithacan Eden world
neither of them doin nothin

that wouldn't make her mama's hair curl

*　　　*　　　*　　　*

The song of the desert is the song of oases
the white sand and midnight blue
of Persian Miniatures

In college I took the Lüscher Color Test
"not a party game" we played
as a party game

The colors you chose showed your balance of mind
the book said and I got four asterisks
which meant not even with psychological counseling
would my mind be right

I saw the cultural bias of course
bright yellow and cool green
being the colors of Switzerland on a nice day

I chose burnt orange and a warm brown
the colors "only refugees" had chosen
the colors of Iranian cliff towns

Third I chose a dark blue
which meant according to the book
I used sex to block my fears
of various underworlds and my sense of doom

O well

The pipes of Pan play

as the pipes of Pan do

And it was a midnight blue

the color of oases

the cry of loons

*   *   *   *

In a glaze of light

the desert men of the high plateau

have faces like worn shoes

Descendents of Alexander's men

their gazes impassive over wide valleys

their stories as cadenced

as Omar Khayyam

Goats jangling like temple bells

they take tea in a circle

talk with their hands

haggling the prices of horses

I know nothing of their wives

or daughters

shadowy sometimes giggly in the doorways

*   *   *   *

No massing of light on a sundown cliff face

was ever more magical than the changing light

in our son's face

The garden gnome crouching at your side
primed to know name and each thrilling step
of each new planting his voice
of query and awe a small
very silvery bell

His little collie Tommy carved trails
into our deep thickets and taught him the woods
quail raccoon an occasional fox
a big black stray he glowered down
like the wrath of God
He died on one of those trails on a sunny day
at just age 10 with a single yelp
Our son's wail like a knife in the heart
lasted forever

What could I teach him the world
is sometimes like a poem but mostly isn't
Distrust moneymen corporate slogans pompous diction

The larger he grew the smaller I seemed

Now he has sideburns like Jim Bowie
and slouches in the sun where he walks

We hope he'll learn to think

*　　　*　　　*　　　*

I wanted to write a poem
whose first line anticipated its last
a box of inevitability
an inevitable box

But life is not like that
Life is a Bob Dylan song
that might go anywhere
or become mumbly and indecipherable

Tramps train whistles a bad sky

We wait for the refrain
Buzzards are circling the bad sky
Tramps enter the train whistles
and then the far blue mountains

But we have faith
Beauty is also circling we think
We wait for the refrain

*   *   *   *

And there you are again in the garden
after long winter and long years
your sports car body our chiropractor
complains you treat like a truck
your mud wife duds a swatch of black earth
glazing your forehead
radiant

pensive

dreaming garden again out of the squalor

of sticks and mud the sprawled

scrawled skeletons

There's no light I'd rather enter

than this sun on our porch in late March

the bare trees on the far hills rusting with inner fires

the lake ice jagged and scarred

and about to vanish

And we could vanish too Love

become wolves on our ancient hill

our tails still plumed and playful

our eyes still fires

a little blood on the sumac leaves

their wands waving toward a new autumn

MARY

(1901-1991)

In that city of black iron lace and Gullah talk,
sin sashaying in shadow, I see you walk
down Pirate's Alley, the quick click of your heels
too Episcopal for the tolling of St. Louis's twelve-tongued bells—
a tea rose in a carnival of azaleas—
white-gloved, sky blue, crisp as your forbearers of East Anglia
yet frankly forgiven in the not quite sultry air
of Easter, taken in by the wide river-mouth patois
of slithering shadows on darkened stairs
in just glimpsed courtyards

and swallowed whole in the black rivers of music,
sirening souls, palaces of jazz-joy, the air thick
with spangled night. A slur of voices
and footfalls on the wet-black streets poised
in mid-summer. Bourbon, Decatur, great
boozy names rolled deep in the throat—
a swill of voices
like the night's breeze, tropical, luscious.
And yours in the plush garden of wrought-iron chairs
crackling like a voice on the wireless—
matter-of-fact as a boot sole,
yet fluttering, fluting its thrill
of the just-so.

You were my first mother in that city of flowering nights
and sweating patios. Duplicitous, cunning,
sometimes mad as a hatter,
you undermined your own daughter
to hold me in the tight
niche of your charms—there where Lafitte
strode and Napoleon's death mask
stared ceilingward, I see you flash—
old outlaw in a city of outlaws,
sainted in a city of saints,
"queers," "reprobates." You gave me awe
and madness, a taste for all things stained

and fallen.
You were my New Orleans,
your chasteness the flip-side of the stripper's martyred gaze,
the sagging wistful gays
your courtiers, the wisteria your bloom.
Mary, they called you. Mary of the crossword puzzle and afternoon
tea, Mary of the rocks, Mary of situations,
whose fall from grace—divorced, shunned,
a bastard grandson and a strident, quick-tongued daughter—
was resurrection in a place of flowers

and music, of terraced talk
on the floating hills of passing nights.
I learned to walk,
your hand in my hand, your electric

voice in my ear.

Even over years, your letters came with the same click

and stutter, your "Angel" signature the relic

of some old family joke

I never quite got.

"The Velvet Bulldozer,"

your doctors whispered near your death.

Your shingles punished you for years,

your retinas detached, your hearing failed.

Only your mind kept ticking in its queer act of will.

In the end, you were vituperative and genteel

as any southern belle. Nurses scuttled.

Doctors deferred. But even their regard

could not hold you forever.

You died with a small sigh—

white in a whited field.

LAMENTATIONS

LAMENT 1

I sat on the edge of my bed and I wailed and I wept
and I wanted to be empty as wind
and avoid all this old man dying shit
all this piecemeal dissolution humiliation
I wanted to rise like the Phoenix like the sun
and be new in the morning like the sun
I wanted to be 56 forever everything still
almost possible you like a mirage
just ahead within reach a rainbow's
shimmering I wanted to walk in
content in my fate to be walking still walking
the ache in my knees both telling and reassuring
and you in the paper tiara from the party
Queen May aswirl in the ribbons of mock death
and resurrection and I knew making love
 to you would make me whole through the universe
and everything else the denouement the terrible denouement
weeping and keening holding the rags the bitter rags
and then I was empty as wind and quiet

LAMENT 2

I went to the place of the poem but it was small
and dark and smelled like the ancient dens of foxes
Time kept coming back to scratch at the door
Old words littered the walls as if to keep the damp out
Someone had lit a fire but the ashes were cold
and the spiders were everywhere
And there was such sadness in the spaces between words
so much nothingness in the everything they said
Why fear the nothingness but we do
How fear the meaninglessness which we are
Here is my voice hang it on a tree
Here is my shoe which remembers me
And beautiful were your black diamonds
like the beauty of the sea at night
the points and spires and breezes of the night
where you passed and I followed and the words went out
and I vanished

LAMENT 3

I wanted to steal the last word from Death I suppose
and the silkiest of thefts are the poems of moonlight
poems of the sea and vast deserts their premonitions
And yet the Angel of Death is all kindness we're told
leading us out into moonlight through cracks in the clouds
had we known had we listened as the terrible talons
of pain and undoing let go
                                    let us pray let us hope
the last ravening moments no end of consciousness
but a beginning let us hope let us pray
though your buttocks domes against my limp gizmo
are all I need tonight to shore me home

LAMENT 4

How shall I say goodbye to myself poor
Charles Bon in his New Orleans and his emptiness
his decadence and charm and poisonous knowledge
who yet found you beyond all luckiness or fate
Goodbye to the heart hurt by its own betrayals
the mind full of inconsequence and error
a voice too full of itself
knickknacks and charms and the color blue
the silent cries of trees and the lake's sheen
and the numberless leaves haunting the numbered days
The man of the hour is the skeleton in the sombrero
who lies down in the curves of the voluptuous señorita
to a clatter of bedpans in the wings and the cackling of the damned
I sang you the songs of your fiery bones
and the soft opening flower of a dying kiss
Farewell to the grief of days and the holy smell of roses
your face knees voice like water
thighs like snow and eyes full of sky
Your laugh startled me so so long ago
My will such as it is I give to clouds and to dreaming
my bones to the cathedrals of sand
to the pottery shards of lost places
my eyes to the vulture who resembles me
my wishes to wind and my loneliness
to thousand year old trees and the deserts of desire
I loved you in the simplest of ways my girl
and this is my poem which has no ending

LAMENT 5

I can imagine the loneliness of widows unraveling
unwelcoming days and old men in shut rooms
measuring their meds losing their minds dates names
If only vanishing were easy an old movie maybe
the corny deathbed speech the melodrama
each bedside mourner a cameo and case study
You see in it the eyes the soul speaking eye
to eye for the last time drinking the last horizon
And the faces strange and the rooms we wake in
with a start the floor moving and the windows dark
are no more ours than the clouds are or the voices of children
Is it the book misplaced that makes me weep
or tortured animals slaughtered children rape
by bayonet or any gone world's going
My grandmother kept a book 85 years pressing
a four-leaf clover given by a friend when they were five
Isn't that worth more than walking on the moon
but nothing stays still straight or in place
but the mute dignity of bones
bones without memory bones without song
So let us go under the hill and over the sky
and let us be bones together

ANCIENT MUSIC

All-ee All-ee In Come Free

All-ee All-ee Outs In Free

Ollie Ollie Oxen Free

Ourselves our secrets released from hairy shadows Mother trees
we came bewitched by stars and insect scratchings
We were ghosts made of black mist
We were silent as stones
We had no faces
loud hearts
We felt steely and cruel
like Greeks on a night raid
We came floating like fireflies
toward a language only half our own
Our fathers smelled like Scotch
our mothers like strange flowers
We came lightly padding on our dark animal souls
who knew vanishing was an art
and returning was easy

All-ee All-ee in come free
All-ee All-ee outs in free
Ollie Ollie oxen free